NELSON'S NEW WEST INDIAN READERS

INTRODUCTORY BOOK 2

REVISED EDITION

CLIVE BORELY

Illustrated by LYNNE WILLEY

OXFORD

UNIVERSITY PRESS

OXFORD

UNIVERSITY PRESS

Great Clarendon Street, Oxford, OX2 6DP, United Kingdom

Oxford University Press is a department of the University of Oxford.
It furthers the University's objective of excellence in research, scholarship,
and education by publishing worldwide. Oxford is a registered trade mark of
Oxford University Press in the UK and in certain other countries

First published by Thomas Nelson and Sons Ltd in 1974
Second edition published by Nelson Thornes Ltd in 1988
This edition published by Oxford University Press in 2015

British Library Cataloguing in Publication Data
Data available

978-0-17-566357-6

10 9

Printed by Multivista Global Ltd

Acknowledgements

Although we have made every effort to trace and contact all
copyright holders before publication this has not been possible in all
cases. If notified, the publisher will rectify any errors or omissions at
the earliest opportunity.

Links to third party websites are provided by Oxford in good faith
and for information only. Oxford disclaims any responsibility for
the materials contained in any third party website referenced in
this work.

Note to the Teacher

Introductory Books 1 and 2 constitute the second half of the **Nelson New West Indian Readers** programme intended for infant departments of primary schools. **Infant Books 1 and 2,** the first half of the programme, are based on a phonic approach to the teaching of reading to which certain elements of 'look and say' and other methods have been added. The **Introductory Books** continue this phonic approach, and you are reminded that the suggestions made in the **Infant Books** need to be continued. The **Introductory Books** do not have the appearance of phonic texts. This is because the phonic rules covered in **Infant Books 1 and 2** have made it possible to generate a wide vocabulary which can be used without the unnatural rhyming sentences which are a feature of many phonic readers.

The first three pages of **Introductory Book 1** are written to recall the characters of the **Infant Books** and give pupils a feeling of confidence in the new readers.

The new material in the **Introductory Books** takes the young reader into words of two and three syllables. The first step is taken with the introduction of the past tense form of the verb, e.g. **look – looked; like – liked,** etc. You should first revise the uninflected form of all the verbs on the page, reminding the class of the phonic rules they might have forgotten. Then you should show how '-ed' when added to these words indicates past tense. The class should then be made to read the words in pairs: **look – looked; like – liked,** etc. You should point out how, with words ending in 'y', the 'y' changes to 'i' before the '-ed' is added. The 'ow' sound as in **cow** should be introduced in the same way as was done in the **Infant Books,** along with its alternative spelling 'ou'. Children should be taught the sound 'owl' as a unit, and then combined with different initial consonants. With 'ou', they can be taught this sound and then made to pronounce the words in stages, e.g., **ou – lou – loud.** The lengthening 'e', and the 'alk' which were used in the **Infant Books** are practised here as well.

The other rules introduced in **Introductory Book 1** are 'oo' as in **pool;** 'or' as in **port,** the final 'sh' as in **hush,** and the '-er' suffix as in **run – runner, teach – teacher;** the '-al' and '-le' as in **medal** and **handle;** the '-er', '-est' suffix of the comparative and superlative (**fast, faster, fastest**) of adjectives; and the '-ist' suffix as in **cycle – cyclist.**

Introductory Book 2 aims to give further practice in dealing with words of two or more syllables and introduces a number of new 'look and say' words.

You will see that there are few new phonic rules added in the **Introductory Books.** At this stage pupils have learnt the basic rules of single syllable words. They have learnt all the consonant sounds and all the short vowel sounds, and are able to combine these to form words or syllables. They have learnt the long vowel combinations, e.g. 'ai', 'ea', 'ou', and the lengthening 'e' rule.

They have also learnt the major and final consonants, and have been introduced to the suffixes of tense and comparison.

You should now help them to develop the competence and confidence to use these rules readily and to develop the ability to 'work out' and recognise the most frequently used words automatically. This means engaging in such activities as phonic word building by the use of the blackboard or word charts, reading of phrase groups, and the making of short reading passages designed to give practice in specially selected rules for revision. Reading of the lesson in the textbook should not be viewed as the sole or even primary objective of the reading lesson. The child is not being taught **to read a book ,** but **to read.** The stories serve as an incentive to the child and successful reading of them indicates a growth in reading skill, but the teacher must engage in all the preliminary and back-up activities that lead to real mastery of this important skill.

Clive Borely

Our friends Tim, John, Sita and Ann were
   sitting under a mango tree.
Mohan came up.
"Do you know what tomorrow is? It's
   David's birthday."
"Oh, boy!" said John. "I forgot all about it.
   What can we do about it now? It's too
   late to buy him anything."
"We don't have any money anyway," said
   Tim. "We have to do something that does
   not cost money."

"Let's have a picnic by the river. That won't cost much," said Mohan.
"That's a good idea, we can ask our parents to give us a chicken and we can have a barbecue on the river bank," said Ann.
"Right," said Sita, "I'll make a cake and Tim can bring sandwiches."

Ann went to tell her mother about the
　　picnic.
"Can you give us a chicken for the
　　barbecue, please, Mummy?"
"Who is going to cook it?" asked her
　　mother.
"We are," replied Ann.
"You are too young to cook chicken on an
　　open fire. It is not safe."
"Oh, Mummy," cried Ann. "I always look on
　　when you cook, and Joan will help too."

"No, Ann. I can't let you girls and boys try
    to cook on an open fire. Some adult must
    be there. I'll come with you."
At last Ann agreed.
Mr Jones, Tim's father, also came to the
    picnic.
"I'll just come to see that you boys don't
    get into trouble," he said with a smile.

When they got to the river bank Mr Jones
    said, "Do you want to catch some fish?"
"Oh, yes," said the boys.
"But how shall we catch them?"
"We need a net, or a hook and line,"
    said Mohan.
"We did not bring any of those things,"
    said David.

"I'll go back to the house and bring
      something to catch them with," said
      Mr Jones.
Mohan looked down and saw some fishes.
"Look, look! There is a fish," he said.
"Yes, and here is another," said Ann.
"Look, there go some more," said David.
"There are many fishes in this river.
      But how are we going to get them?"
      asked Ann.
They sat down to wait for Mr Jones.
The boys looked at the fishes in the water.

"Look at that pretty fish there," said David.
"Let's get it now. If we wait for Mr Jones it
     will get away," said Ann.
"Oh, no! We can't let it get away,"
     said David.
They sat and waited and looked at the fish.
They all wished that Mr Jones would hurry
     back.

Ann threw a piece of bread in the water.
The fish came to eat it. She threw another
 piece.
  The fish came again.
"Hurry! Hurry! Mr Jones," said Ann.
  "Don't let this pretty fish get away."

shoe	fish	down	bank
shirt	dish	crown	sank
ship	crash	frown	drank
shape	splash	drown	prank

They sat and waited, and looked at the fish.
Then David said, "Throw a piece of bread
    near me. When the fish comes I'll get it."
Ann threw a piece of bread in the water.
The fish came up near to David.

He put his hand in the water to grab it, but
the fish got away.
"Throw another piece," said David.
"I'll catch it this time."
Ann threw another piece of bread in the
water.
The fish came up for it slowly.
David waited. When it was near he tried
to catch it.
And SPLASH!
David fell into the river.
"Help! Help!" cried David.

"Help!" cried Ann. "Run and get
   Mr Jones."
"Hurry! Hurry!" cried Sita. "David fell into
   the river! He will drown. Call Mr Jones.
   Hurry! Hurry!"
Mr Jones ran up.
"What's the matter?" he said.
   "What's going on?"
"Oh, Mr Jones, help David. He is in the
   river. He can't swim. He will drown."
"Hurry! Help David."

Mr Jones jumped into the river and took
    David's arm.
"Come on, David," he said. "Stand up.
    You can stand here. The river is not
    deep."
David stood up. He wanted to cry.
Poor David! All the other children laughed.
"Take off your shirt and your shoes,
    David," said Mr Jones.
"Put them in the sun to dry."
David took off his wet shirt and shoes and
    put them in the sun to dry.

"Come on. Now we have to catch some
   fishes."
Mr Jones had a net and a big jar on the
   bank.
He put some river water in the jar.
"Hold this for me, please," he asked Sita.
He gave her the jar and put the net in the
   water.
Ann threw a piece of bread in the water.
A fish came for it.
Mr Jones pulled up the net slowly.

The fish was caught in it.

Mr Jones put the fish in the jar and went
   back to catch more.

Then David saw the pretty fish.

"Please, Mr Jones," he said. "Let me catch
   it with your net."

Mr Jones gave the net to David. David put it
   in the water and waited. The pretty fish
   saw the bread and swam by slowly.

David pulled up the net.

"There," he said. "I have it."

"You made me fall into the river but
   I caught you," said David to the pretty
   fish.

Just then Ann and Joan called out,
   "Come on, boys, lunch is ready."
The boys put the fish back into the river
   and ran to the spot where Ann and her
   mother were cooking the chicken.
They sat down around a table cloth on the
   grass.
Ann served the chicken and Joan served
   fried breadfruit. It was delicious.
After the meal they sang "Happy Birthday
   to David."
Then suddenly, the rain started to fall.
"Come on," said Ann's mother, "Pick up
   your things. We have to run home."
The picnic was over but the boys and girls
   did not mind.
They had had a good time.

frog	small	start	flag	shop
from	smart	stop	flap	ship
Fred	smell	step	flour	share
friend	smoke	stem	fly	shape
fruit	smooth	still	flow	shoe
until	become			

Liz and Terry are going to their school
   sports meeting.
They want to take some snacks for their
   friends.

"Let's make a big cake to take to the sports
  meeting," said Lizzy.
"We can cut it up and share it with all our
  friends."
"Yes, but let's make some small cup cakes
  instead. Then we won't have to cut it up.
  We can have one each."
"That's a smart idea, Terry," said Lizzy.
"Shall we ask Mummy to help us?"
"No, let's do it ourselves," said Lizzy.

The girls took the flour, sugar, eggs, and
    butter. They started to work.
Lizzy put the sugar and the butter into the
    bowl.
"We have to mix this until it becomes
    smooth," she said.
Terry looked on. Then she said,
    "Let me try. I want to help now."

batter	something	kitchen
better	anything	moment
bitter	happening	somebody
butter	outside	instead
bigger	inside	vanilla

Lizzy passed the bowl to Terry.
Terry held the spoon and turned the batter
  slowly.
"Boy! This is hard work," said Terry.
"Is it smooth yet?"
"No," said Lizzy, "You can still see the
  grains of sugar."

"We have to keep on beating it."
"You do it," said Terry. "I'm tired."
Lizzy smiled.
"Let's add a little milk," she said.
"That will make it softer and easier to
beat."
After a long time the batter became
smooth.
Then the girls added the flour and a few
drops of vanilla essence.

"Boy! That smells good," said Terry.
"Hmm – and tastes good too," said Lizzy,
   licking her fingers.
"Now let's put this batter into the paper
   cups and turn on the oven. The oven
   must be hot before we put the cakes in."
Terry lit the oven and Lizzy filled the cups.
Then they went outside to play.

Joan and Ann were playing outside.
Lizzy and Terry ran to them.
"We're making mud pies for our dolls,"
  Joan told them. "Do you want to make
  some?"

"We have just made some real cup cakes,"
   said Terry.
"Oh, no," said Joan. "Is that true, Lizzy?"
Lizzy smiled and said, "Yes, we have."
Ann said, "I know what happened.
   Your mummy made the cakes and you
   helped."
"Oh, no. We made them ourselves.
   Mummy didn't help.
   She doesn't even know we've done it.
   She's at the book shop."

"Wait," shouted Joan. "I smell
    something burning."
"Yes, I smell it too. It must be
    in the kitchen."
The girls ran into the house.
They ran into the kitchen.
Smoke was coming from the oven.

"Oh, dear! The cakes are burning,"
  said Ann.
At that moment Mother came in.
She opened the oven door. The smoke
  rushed out. When it cleared they
  looked in.
"There was a piece of bread in the oven,"
  said Mother. "Somebody lit the stove
  and burnt the bread."
"Oh, goody," cried Ann. "The cakes are not
  burnt."
"No," said Lizzy. "We haven't put them in
  yet."

At last the sports day arrived.
Mohan was in the first race.
All the runners went to the starting line.
Some stood quietly, others ran up and
  down.
Mr Stone came up. He was the starter.
He said, "Get ready. . .set. . ."
BANG went the starting gun.
The boys raced away.
A little boy was in the lead.
He had started just before the gun.
Behind him was a big bunch of boys.
Our friends looked for Mohan,
  but they could not see him.
He was in the bunch.

Then they saw him. He was fourth!
They shouted, "Go on, Mohan! Go on!"
Mohan started to stride out.
He passed one boy, then another.
Now he was second!
The boys and girls shouted,
   "Go on, Mohan! Go on!"

Mohan tried. He was gaining on the boy,
   but the race was nearly over.
Then, suddenly, the boy in front stumbled
   and Mohan passed him.
The little boy came second.
The boys and girls shouted and jumped in
   the air.
Then they ran to Mohan and hugged him.
They were all very happy.

The next race was for girls.
Joan and Sita were both running.
Lizzy, Judy, Ann and the boys
   stood near the finishing line.
They wanted to see the end of the race.
They wanted their friends to win.
The girls were getting ready for the race.
They crouched and waited for the gun.

Then Sita and Joan dashed off before the
    gun.
The starter called them back and spoke
    to them.
Then they got ready again.
This time Joan was the last to start.
She was too careful.
She did not want to make another false
    start.
Sita was out in front.
The boys and girls jumped for joy.
But another girl passed her.
The boys and girls shouted, "Run, Sita!
    Run, Joan!"

Joan was running well.
She was passing those ahead of her with
  ease.
Sita kept on running, but she could not
  catch the leader.
At the end of the race Sita was second,
  and Joan was fourth.
Everyone was sorry for Joan.
If only she had not started badly,
  she might have won.
Joan was sad, but not for long.
Miss James came to her and said,
  "Well run, Joan. You put up a great fight.
  I really liked that."
Joan felt pleased.
"I'll try again next year," she said.
  "That's right, Joan. I'm sure you will do
  better next time." Miss James smiled
  and handed her an ice-cream cone.

The other boys and girls were not so
   successful.
John fell and scratched his knee.
David sprained his ankle.
But Tim made everybody scream with
   laughter.
He was in the bun race.
All the runners had their hands tied
   behind their backs.
A bun was tied to a string and hung in front
   of each runner.
The boys had to eat the bun first,
   and then run to the finish line.

When the race started, Tim tried to take
    a big bite of his bun.
The bun swung away from him.
When it swung back, he tried again.
This time he missed.
The bun hit him in the eye.
Everybody was laughing at Tim now.
He waited for the bun to return.
This time he opened his mouth wide,
    leaned forward, and bit!

He caught the bun in his teeth,
  and fell on the ground with it.
He rolled on his back,
  and tried to eat the bun.
But it slipped from his mouth,
  and fell to the ground.
Mr Stone, the starter, came up to Tim
  and lifted him off the ground.
He told the others to get on with the race.
But the crowd was not interested
  in the race any more.
Everyone had laughed enough at Tim.
Tim ran back to his group of friends.
He was a little sad, but not for long.
Lizzy gave him an extra cup cake
  for his great try.
Like Joan, he was happy now.

The Sports Day was over.
The children were returning home
   from the school ground.
"I'm glad the Sports Day is gone,"
   said Sam. "Now we don't have to go
   running in the afternoons any more."
"You never went running," said Joan.
   "Except that day when the dog stole your
   sandwich."

"I know," he replied. "But everybody else
did. And I had no one to talk to."
"Now we don't have to run
and we can't think what to do,"
said John.
Just then the children passed the front
of a new book shop.

"Look! The new book shop is open,"
    said Sita.
She was always happy when she went
    into a book shop. There were so many
    new books.
They all looked so exciting and interesting.
"Let's go in," she said.
"Look at this book on space travel,"
    said John.
"I like these story books," said Ann.

"Here is one about how to make magic."
"I want to be a magician," said John.
He picked up a ruler from the shelf and
   said, "I am the great Lorenzo, master
   magician. I command you to turn into a
   mouse!"
He waved his hand and it knocked
   a toy box off the shelf.
It fell with a bang to the floor.
The cover came off and out of the box ran a
   toy mouse.

The children looked at the toy mouse in
    surprise.
Then they started to laugh. John began to
    laugh, too.
"I knew it! I knew it!" he said. "I am a great
    magician."
The manager of the shop came up.
"What's all this noise about!" he said.
    "Who threw that box down?"
"The great Lorenzo," replied Sita.
The children started to laugh,
but the manager was angry.

"I'm sorry," said Joan. "We didn't mean
   any harm. It was all a mistake. But it was
   very funny. We'll put the box back in its
   place."
"All right," said the manager.
"As long as nothing is broken."
The girls packed away the box
   with the toy mouse.

"I think we ought to buy something,"
said Sita. "Then the manager
won't be so angry."
"Yes," said Tim. "I want this book
about great sportsmen."
"We can't buy that," said Mohan.
"It costs too much. Let's buy something
cheaper."
"I don't have any money," said Ann.
"I spent all mine at the sports ground."
"So did I," said John.
"Then we can't buy anything," said Mohan.
"We'll have to come back another time."

The children started to leave. They said
"Goodbye" to the manager and walked
to the door.
"Wait," said the manager. "I'm sorry I was
angry with you. Here's a little gift for you
as it's our opening day."
He gave them each a balloon, a colouring
book, and a box of crayons.
"Oh, thank you, sir," they shouted,
and ran home with their presents.

Word List

before	return	better	paper
behind	receive	letter	finger
because	recall	fatter	laughter
behold	repeat	matter	starter

another	nearly	stumble
outside	clearly	humble
ourselves	badly	grumble
something	sadly	fumble
careful	gladly	nimble
everything	hopefully	dimple
everybody	madly	simple

vanilla	together	Caribbean
suddenly	resemble	Tobago
finishing	imitate	Trinidad
successful	department	
happening		

I	make	bread	everybody
you	go	cake	sometimes
we	run	to school	
they	eat	a picture	
some people	see	birds singing	
my parents	hear	an errand	
		home	

he	makes	bread	at some time
she	goes	cake	everyday
Peter	eats	to school	
Jane	sees	to work	
everybody	hears	an errand	
	runs	a picture	

I	made	bread	last week
you	went	cake	yesterday
he	ate	to school	last year
she	saw	to walk	a few minutes ago
it	hear	a picture	
we	ran	a song	
they		an errand	
my parents			
Peter and James			
Mary and Ann			